The Black Plac

The Black Place

Tamar Yoseloff

Seren is the book imprint of
Poetry Wales Press Ltd.
57 Nolton Street, Bridgend, Wales, CF31 3AE
www.serenbooks.com
facebook.com/SerenBooks
twitter@SerenBooks

The right of Tamar Yoseloff to be identified as
the author of this work has been asserted in accordance
with the Copyright, Designs and Patents Act, 1988.

© Tamar Yoseloff, 2019.

ISBN: 978-1-78172-559-7
ebook: 978-1-78172-564-1

A CIP record for this title is available from the British Library.

The publisher acknowledges the financial assistance of the Welsh Books Council.

Cover artwork: 'Black Place IV' (1944) by Georgia O'Keeffe
© Georgia O'Keeffe Museum/DACS 2019.

Cover design: Andrew Lindesay

Author photograph: Stephen Wells

Printed in Bembo by Severn, Gloucester.

Contents

The C Word	9
Dawn	10
Girl	11
Alice in Hell	12
Anti-midas	13
The Lambeth Prophecy	14
Basement	15
In Clover	16
Train at Night in the Desert	17
Bearskull	18
The Treasury of Alonis	19
Redaction 1	20
Heart Burn	21
Walk All Over Me	22
Emoji	23
City	24
Occupation Road	25
Sheeple	26
Holiday Cottage	27
The Wayfarer	28
Snails	29
Islanders	30
Night Mode	31
Redaction 2	32
Disappointment	33
Body Language	34
Little Black Dress	35
Climacteric	36
Jade	37
Absent Friends	39
Frits De Vries's Great Work	40
Darklight	41

Small White Dot   44
Nephritic Sonnet   45
Redaction 3   46
Cuts   47
The Black Place   54

Notes   56
Acknowledgements   58

The Black Place was the name Georgia O'Keeffe gave to one of her favorite painting sites, located in the Bisti Badlands in Navajo country, about 150 miles northwest of her home in Ghost Ranch. It was a stretch of desolate gray and black hills that the artist said looked from a distance like "a mile of elephants."

Isolated far off the road and away from all civilization, O'Keeffe made several camping trips there in the 1940s, with her assistant Maria Chabot. Writing to Alfred Stieglitz in 1944, the year Black Place II was made, Chabot described in words what O'Keeffe captured in paint: "... the black hills — black and grey and silver with arroyos of white sand curving around them — pink and white strata running through them. They flow downward, one below the next. Incredible stillness!"

from georgiaokeeffe.net

When I was sick they moved me to a room with a window and suddenly through the window I saw two fir trees in a park, and the grey sky, and the beautiful grey rain, and I was so happy. It had something to do with being alive.

Joan Mitchell

The C Word

catches in the throat; the first syllable
on its own, enabling, followed by a hissing snake,
rattletail bringing up the rear.

It trumpets its presence in the glare of the ward,
sneaks into glossy brochures, flashes its statistics
(the odds are against me), looks like *carer* but isn't.

Not to be confused with the other c word
that cuts at both ends, detonated in hate
murmured in love – how can it be both?

And how can I contain them, sites of birth
and death? I should know how to speak
of what's inside me. To be blunt.

Dawn

The city stirs, planes drown out birds,
the fox cries like a strangled child

over the uncertain street. Not a soul.
Each day I lose more: words,

names, things I thought I cared about.
The sun does its duty, as it should

but dawn still holds on to night
like a blanket covering a body.

Poppies stamp the lawn, loud as fists,
but their petals are widow's skin.

I'll lie down in their red caress, let them
stroke my cheek, black eyes winking.

Girl

comes from nowhere, no great shakes –
a slip, a trick, a single polka dot
dancing on her own. In the swoosh

of the train she is gone, to trip
the switch of her heart, to fill the gap –
mind you, she's been there before

and it sucks. She's stuck on night shift,
flashing her dugs, doing her bit
and for what? No one

gets it – she holds her tongue
but slippy lizard can't be tamed,
sliding over cusses, tequila, semen.

She's good for nothing because nothing's
good: sirens drown out violins
and crows swoop to carnage in the street.

Alice in Hell

And then the White Queen said
off with her head!

Down the hole I went,
plunged into a throbby gullet;
crocodile tears spiked my arms,
drew rubies, price of my dewy flesh.

That infernal rabbit kept muttering
you're late, you're late, and in a beat
I knew I was dead, but not
in the pearly place.

The Hatter, murderer of time,
wielded the second hand
like a stiletto, rosy juice flew
through the picket pikes on my skin,

my mouth swilled rare claret,
thick elixir of my heart. I longed
to wake, caught in the crease
between sleep and slump,

the cat's grin taunting,
the rabbit's satin paw pressed
on my breast, my breath
in his fist.

Anti-midas

Everything he touches turns to shit:

silver sucked of its glitter, bankrupt;
smooth skin shriveled, breasts sapped.

He balls his fists in his pockets,
but his eyes spread garbage in the flowers,

his stare sinks joy, his cesspit heart
seeks the charred core of the sun.

He tries to run, but his feet have slabbed
to stone, he is halted in the mire

of hatred. This is the world he's made,
although he's quick to pass the mantle

to the next man – his curse, his disease.
He breeds dirt from dirt,

his cry is a wheeze in the dark:
Help me. Dig me out.

The Lambeth Prophecy

In ancient rain, tender gardens
stripped, I'm caught in the drag
of giant girders, soon another
luxury city view.
         Unkind asphalt
jams my toes as I spring verticals,
rise higher and higher
through dissected sky

to find there *is* a God,
at least a guy who'd buy a round
for the lads outside The Pineapple,
his labours halted, at rest.

                      Progress.
Razing, sweeping clean.
I must take stock: the oak, the echoing
green, before I gutter, stumble
drunk.
         The quick buck backs
the trend. This season it's Dismal Grey
as in battleship, storm cloud, steel.

My days are numbered: little boxes
multiply over the city's face
while I labour at the boundary fence.

Basement

Bodiless feet pass the window,
hot tar holds the soles of their shoes.

The forecourt bouquet
frets in its makeshift vase (plastic bottle sliced in half).

Nature, cut and dry, a tribute framed by brick:
why try to keep it alive?

Leaves curl, clasping a rose's balled bloom; still
life clinging to its scant stem.

A single petal detaches, drops
without drama.

In Clover

That if any man walking in the fields find any foure-leaved grasse,
he shall in a small while after find some good thing
– Sir John Melton

She has enough to fill a case the length of the hall.
Years of tuning her eye to difference, inhabiting
the caterpillar's miniature domain. Always a strange girl.

One leaf is sunshine, the second is rain.

When Eve was banished from Eden, she snatched one,
a souvenir of Paradise. Or so they say. No doubt she left
with nothing, but we like the idea of a small green hope.

Browned petals like the skin of old ladies.

They say the bearer can spy fairies, banish evil spirits;
four is the number of the Cross. We stash away our charms,
remembering the rabbit's foot wasn't lucky for the rabbit.

Crushed to dust in time.

She started when she was seven. An auspicious number.
The casual hunt grew to obsession as she got older.
And now she can't face the world before her, only

the ground we will all go to.

Train at Night in the Desert

Charcoal dark. Nothing to see but twin ghosts
of your face in safety glass, the man opposite
upholstered in thick fibres of slumber.

You're pulled by a faith
in steel. The train is a lung breathing dust
as it huffs to a black dot on the map:
a bug stuck on its back, giggly legs flailing in air.

Out there, the coyote keeps its secrets,
it has its own line of action.
It doesn't give a shit about your plans.

Bearskull

My uncle was a recreational hunter.
His house was crammed with the skins and skulls
of his kills. Jackrabbits, bighorn sheep, wild cats,
black bears. He fashioned ashtrays out of hooves.
All his rugs had heads.

There's a photo of his wife, her pale hair
falling over her face, a hint of a smile,
with a grizzly stuck in mock attack behind her.
The bear reaches out as if to hold her close
in his furry paws.

She couldn't stand all those glass eyes staring:
it's either them or me.

I lift the skull from the box with both hands:
did the bear rear when the shot hit, his huge head
swaying side to side, dead brush crushed
as he fell? Did my uncle feel the chamber's release,
the bullet forced towards the bear's heart?

The sky closed around them, bear and man;
the air sang with the stink of meat.

My uncle never thought his wife would go first;
she was so much younger. He paced the bare rooms
she'd redecorated in French Provincial style
with swirls of flowers and fruit,
lost in his own house.

The Treasury of Alonis

To pine means to yearn, this is what we do,
on a hill above the sea where Romans prayed
to equinoctial deities.

What do we mean when we say we have faith?

At the temple site the ditch fills with plastic bottles, Coke cans
for our descendants to excavate.
Will they conclude this was the start of our decline?

Divers sweep the sea floor where a merchant ship sank,
cargo intact: amphorae packed with garum. We stuff our mouths
with *boquerones,* wipe our salty lips, call the waiter for more wine.

To pine is to lament what we don't have, what we lost –
trees cling to the cliff edge,
our fingers are sticky with resin.

What do we mean when we say we've lost our faith?

The goddess could occupy a pocket, fit a hand;
her owner kept her close. Only her head survives.
Her hair is waved like the sea. In her glass case we see our reflection.

And in this case, the bones of a soldier, plain as the grave.
His remains can tell us how he lived, how he died.
Can we excavate his soul?

The women wore amulets of gold, element of eternity.

To pine is to ache, to waste away.
It isn't skin that keeps us whole.

The symptoms

come and go

Sometimes you won't be

you should tell your doctor

high

high

high

will have already spread

lungs, liver, brain and bones.

You must see your doctor

Heart Burn

Sweet you say
like I'm a princess or a puppy.
Candy to a baby.

Your face floods my eyes,
a drunk sun, glistening
and ugly.
       I'm done
with gorging on your jaggery
gob, the sticky air around you.

No matter how many times
I spit you out, you refuse to go,
gag my throat.
       Your promise melts
to a bright pool on a hot street.
Suck it up you say.

Walk All Over Me

For you I'd sleep with the worms
just to feel the tread of your heel.

I'd slip on a slapstick peel,
master the fall for your laugh.

I'd super-shrink my dimensions,
wasting is a form of perfection.

I'm the road that loves the rover
so walk all over me –

I love your dirty sole, your holy toe,
the slurp and suck of rubber.
Your heart's in your shoe as you leave.

Make me your shag pile, your Twister dot,
the green sprig of spring
you'll squelch underfoot.

Emoji

The steaming turd that sees and speaks,
subbing for the banana peel beneath
my feet. He's stuck on me; I can't seem
to shake him. So I fire the heavy guns –
the dancing pig, the bow-tied duck.
All in fun.
        But he's got inside my head,
behind my eyes, doesn't need reality
to thrive. The street pixilates, disneyfies;
everyone has purple hair, pop-out eyes,
I can't remove these clown shoes
from my feet, nor the big dumb smile
that's smacked my lips. I dream
of grey, of urban sprawl, in all
its stupendous misery.

City

after Angel Gonzalez

The city is shiny like a toy.
Skyscrapers conquer trees.
Streets are diamond hard.
And then you, amid the jumble of cables.
The sun is my necklace,
I carry your image inside it.
When glass hides spies in plain sight
Facades are futile.
My eyes are too full.
And then you, somewhere far away.
I never said goodbye.
Nothing is left of your presence.
The city polishes its surfaces,
It has no use for us.

Occupation Road

We had enough for a couple of weeks, tins of beans, tins of fruit. We tried to pass the time although all the clocks had stopped. We shuffled cards, their flat patterns and quaint queens soothing. We built transistors from scratch but they picked up nothing but hiss. Everything tasted of tin; I worried it was coming from inside me. You were certain they'd erect cities on our garbage, write sagas in a language we'd never live to speak. The train stammered over the tracks at dusk, cargo scuttling to the far districts.

Sheeple

The train slows to a halt in some shire
or other. The heartland. Lower Slaughter.

Two of them, like cumulus on stilts,
perform a moonwalk in reverse, step

by courtly step, before they charge,
almost lifting off, crashing head to head

and then again, hard-wired to the bunt.
Wars of the flock? Dick fight? Tense détente?

What ticks in their spongy brains?
The rest chew cud, footrot rooting them,

the green and pleasant place of no escape.
They ruminate in marshy gas, while all the birds

of Oxfordshire and Gloucestershire
feast on their creep.

Holiday Cottage

Rain saddens brick, a sodden blackbird
huddles under shrubs. We hunker down
in the stygian kitchen, where even
the knives don't shine.

We're stuck to the window in wait
for sun. It's forecast on the app;
but the sky turns crow-dark, horrorshow.
There's nowhere to go, even home

is sunk, the motorway stacked with
failed daytrippers, sopping girl guides.
The burger van has buggered off.
Trains wade in the wrong kind of rain.

We stare at the knock-off Hay Wain
hung crooked over the hearth
and dream of England: the shire bells,
the box set, the M&S biscuit tin,

the empire we'll never find again;
detained in this hole, this crease
in the map, neither here nor there,
a leave to remain.

The Wayfarer

Here is a sunless land where pigs rejoice
in filth, the man without a pot to piss in
waters the wall at the Sign of the Goose
(the house of ill repute), the dog eyes me

as a potential leg to bite. They can't know
what I've gandered in my time on the road:
buckets of sorrow slopping over, the hard
stare of starvation. I am bone lean. Stooped.

If I look familiar, fellow wanderer,
it's because you see yourself in the mirror
of my eye. You know each step on the path
to the grave is pitted with little deaths.

The gate ahead is locked, so where to go?
I could shelter in the bawd's roofless hovel
beside her ruined crones, or I could fling
the dog these tired bones; the owl knows

the worth of waiting, mouse in its crosshatch eyes;
I'm not as wise − a cat who's trashed eight lives,
its pelt a feast for maggots. God looked down
and spat, so the rain came to these quarters

and will not cease − Noah's flood made swamp.
I'll lay my head on the unforgiving earth
to call a halt to moving, but there's no rest −
sleep is just another dark to fear.

Snails

Withdrawn from toxic sprays, deadly beer,
they aestivate, motionless, in grave homes,
a vital straitening;
                              holed up for days,
ignoring the radio, the funereal newsreader,
we dine on their gummy bodies, tight knots
we prod from shells with little forks
then dip in garlic butter, dangling them
before our mouths
                              leaving only
a hard case, an empty offering:
the spiral's apex – a whirlwind uncoiling.

Islanders

We maroon ourselves
on tiny plots, worlds
shrunk to fit. Our terrain

is difficult, our waves
choppy. We have few
natural resources, we live

on what we forage,
hoard air and water.
We grow turf, hide

in the long grass
so no one can find us,
develop thousand-yard

stares, our eyes fixed
on the horizon, waiting
for a ship that never docks,

the off-island always beyond
reach, always in sun,
like a gem behind glass.

We put seas between us,
we won't be rescued.

Night Mode

The hours are counting
certainty on tiny screens.
I'm turned to silent.

Hair grows faster in the dark
when no one's watching.
I can hear it break through skin.

Cats disappear in boxes
again and again in slow motion.
This is what passes for entertainment.

Say you're *in transit* – it sounds better.
Say you believe in indeterminancy.
No wrong answers just poor questions.

It's already morning in Australia.
How exhausting. Someone is always
crowing about clear blue sky.

Failure is a beautiful word,
the way it curls around the tongue.
Embrace it. Let it love you.

Enough. We'll call it a day.

can

you   see it,

can   you feel a

low

o

oo   o

there may be

loss

32

Disappointment

sticks, a sour kiss. The gold statuette is tin
beneath her nicks.

My stand is to sit
as ice breaks in my glass.

Hours pass

        when Nothing is King. This is the life
I assembled from the kit – not like the picture
on the box.
        Words are black blocks: we say
'orange' or 'train' but their things slip away, flat
on the tongue.

My stand is to stand
as the house falls around me:
cardboard and spit, holes for windows.

Dust settles.
I fit the empty frame.

Body Language

The girl poses for the camera –

in fact for the photographer, let's say the man she loves,
his camera, a machine to translate his gaze:
this is how he sees her, how he's always seen her.

Whatever else has occurred, will occur
in her life, in the world, now
she is content, youth
fixed on gloss, while the days
move with a speed that surprises them
as the shutter's parting lets the light in;

a shadow passes over her skin
like a veil over a widow, a curtain over a window,
in negative her lights dim

and she will be consigned to paper, brittle truth:
a girl he loved once, a girl he carries in his pocket like a charm.

Little Black Dress

Too tight, too short, it weathered nights on the lash
with my broken-spined Plath, my Bacardi & Coke:
a classic LBD from Bendel's or Saks, sole owner
deceased, her closet dispatched to the charity shop
where we picked over Givenchy like vultures;
my wardrobe belonged to the dead – *le smoking*
in sharkskin, a bouclé *veste* with leopard lapels
that died for my sins, which were minor enough
to dress for the part, Rachmaninov oozing
through speakers, the record skipping into dusk,
and us, university girls with daddies and trusts,
drunk and disorderly, dropping off bar stools one
by one, until the time arrives for widow's weeds
and weeping veils, Ray-Bans darkening the sun.

Climacteric

Now I arrive, late
on a frozen sea. Distant glints
mark habitation: a barren
hillside dotted with breeze blocks
where happiness smacks of youth.

Here I'll make do, reinvent myself
from scraps and songs
while poised on a balcony,
a distant marble goddess.

I might as well dance
to appease the monsters.
Once they demanded respect;
now they're old, a bit frayed,
they suck light, rust the past.

Jade

Fine and smooth and cold
but against the flesh it fires,

old stone, healer for what fails,
death can't pale its lustre,

dredged from the river to make
objects of desire: a likeness

of the Buddha, belly polished
to a shine with many wishes;

or a tomb suit stitched with gold,
sized to fit its wearer, passed away –

until his past returns, dredged up
with grave goods: dagger and idol,

his city idyll, built to skim clouds,
gone to ground, gone for good.

*

In this whorl of green a world,
mineral galaxy, nephrite bright –

her beads, passed down to me,
I warm them against my neck,

my breathing body yanked back
from death – I've never prayed

but in these spheres they say
is heaven, unfathomable ocean;

if nothing more they bind me
to her, flesh of her flesh,

perhaps even in disease, a slow
release in her body, passed down,

down – now she is ash and bone
I take what I must take.

★

The circle serves to fascinate –
we move in and out of world

linked by love, the steady clock
of our hearts. She and I stood

before the emperor's new suit,
his last, guessing its weight, heavy

enough to keep his body under,
while his soul flew to wherever

souls escape. She is no place now,
but her things occupy my space:

this jade, colour of what you see
when you look deep in water,

like reaching through the sky
to hold a little piece of earth.

Absent Friends

Portraits should be like memorials – Howard Hodgkin

More colour becomes necessary as time goes
on, and I try to recall the shade of the afternoon
when we sauntered around in next-to-nothing,
sunburnt, a little hungover. There were interiors
with dramatic drapery and bowls of plums
like a parody of Matisse. We passed
the time doing nothing, thinking time was
infinite, but as time marches, whatever
that expression is, I find I'm hoarding
sticks and stones, worthless really; they stand in
for a place I won't revisit, a touch from a lover,
dead now – accumulated junk, assembled
with a cold curator's hand on the mantel.
Do I have the courage for orange:
full-on, juicy, a riot on the canvas, butting up
against true blue, like the Med in July?
Or the real pink of flesh, not Rubenesque,
but dirtier, a smudge of black in the mix,
like your limbs beneath the sheets – the rough
with the smooth? The frames are baroque:
scrolled and curlicued, the sort of thing
we liked in the day, when we thought ourselves
grand, sailing across the parquet after rain,
shaking ourselves off with a sense of importance.
Now I spoil them, paint pooling like blood,
clogging their leaves and buds, so the picture
spills over, and I can't see where it ends
or where they've gone, those absent friends,
in the swirl and turbulence. I keep them
with me in my head where they will always
be found, even though the scene dims,
loses definition, and it's only a matter
of time before I enter the final room,
gloom of night around me, and I hear you
whisper *don't look back.*

Frits De Vries's Great Work

One day, Frits De Vries stopped painting.
It had been a successful career, but there was no satisfaction;
he'd come to the end of what paint could say for him.

He began to collect objects salvaged from the war,
found amid junk in the *vlooienmarkt* or offered in the classifieds.
The owners wanted rid of them; they brought back bad times:

rusted helmets, gas masks, uniforms, empty shells,
battered machine guns, medals, tattered Stars of David
that Jews were forced to sew on their lapels.

Objects took possession of his studio, filled it to the ceiling, slowly
began to infiltrate his house. He couldn't stop them. His wife declared
she no longer wished to sleep besieged by misery.

When Frits died, his treasury was removed piece by piece, shipped
to Guislain Asylum, where the Doctor had gathered his own collection –
art created by inmates. Only madness could stockpile

so many implements that spell evil. His calling was to keep them alive
rather than killing them with paint;
museums were cluttered with enough bowls of fruit.

We stand at the threshold of his rooms, enshrined behind Perspex,
while his things shrug off light, shed function and word,
reveal their greying arrangement.

Darklight

1.

A shooting star makes a sound like a scratch in vinyl,
like the night is a record you can play. Some songs
only make sense when they stutter on a note.
The air is heavy and smells of violets.
The sky is a graveyard of stars.
My eyes hurt from too much looking.

Once I saw the aurora from a dock in Norway.
Men were going about their business, hauling
great loads from one bay to another.
The aurora was nothing to them, it had lost
its wonder. It was green and strange, it swayed
to an unheard tune. It must be what people see

when they think they're haunted, a light that moves
like we do, but has no form. When people come back
from near death, they talk about a pulsing light
at the end of a long hall. I practise my ghost walk,
for when I need to haunt; I am all soft edges,
a silhouette caught on the horizon.

2.

The artist waits until the dead hour, when his eyes
yield to darkness. Only now can he draw, the burden
of sight lifted. He rises from sleep, takes a nub of charcoal,
firm and dry between his fingers, hears its churr against paper,
digs a line into the coarse weave. He wants to be nothing more
than motion, not even a hand, something without source;
he wants to make a mark that doesn't resemble anything
he knows, no word assigned to it. He wants to draw loss –
like a gush of air released through a long-unopened door,
like the way night sucks shape and colour from the chair or rug,
even though he knows they're still here. He can't be certain;
things are unmade in darkness. His body has vanished,
just ticking organs, a funnel of breath. Walls melt away;
the room opens to sky. Faith unravels like a ball of string.

3.

I stand inside a pool of streetlight, holding the dark
at bay – this must be what it's like to have a god.
Sodium casts a sickly yellow on my skin.

In the ancient map there are monsters
hugging the places where the maker
had no clue, where you might fall off the edge

into nowhere. I had a night light as a child,
a plug-in candle in the corner of my room.
But a monster lived behind my eyes,

and even though it died each morning,
it rose up again at bedtime. Back then
my parents would sing me to sleep;

now they're ash and bone. Our lives are brief
like the banks of candles in cathedrals,
each a flame for someone loved;

or the light I see framed in curtained windows:
for each one who's lit a lamp, made a strike
against the dark.

Small White Dot

Cronkite's face blizzards, sucked into static
as the solid-state TV shuts off with a clunk . . .
I'd watch the screen go black, a small white dot
like an eye watching me back as if Cronkite
was still there behind the screen, waiting
for the cathode ray to fire up. He ghosted me
in his death mask, bringing napalm to dinner.

I'm lying on a gurney in theatre; the nurse says
count down from ten. A small white dot
floats above; I lift my arm, hand open, to catch it,
but it's shrinking, smaller, smaller, smaller –
I don't want to let it go, be gone.

I have the power to switch the set back on,
to breathe in, out, in, out, in

Nephritic Sonnet

I wear an oxygen moustache, hating the cold
creep of air into my lungs, but the nurse says
I must keep breathing. I watch the slow clock
of blood through the IV tube, my insides out,
on display, my 'fluid being', my 'wine of life' –
but why would I try to make a poem of this?
I'm nothing more than a few sheets clipped
to a board, my bodily functions monitored
in words that doctors register above my head.
There's no poetry in the hospital gown, worn
thin from the rub of skin, or the urine stench
or how a person dies, without elegy or dirge,
on the other side, just a curtain between us

███████████████████████████

████████████████ blood ███████████████████
████████████████████████████████████

███████████████████████████████
██████████████ blood ██████████████████████
██

██
█████████████

██████████████████████████████████████
██████████████████████████████████████
██████████████████████████████████████
██████████████████████████████████████

█████████████████████████████

███████████████████████████████████████
███████████████████████████████████████
███████████████████████████████████████
███████████████████████████████████████
██ blood ██████████████████████████████████
███████████████████████████████████████
████████████████████████████ blood ████████
████████

█████████ blood █████████████ blood █████████
██████████████████████████████████████
██████████████████████ blood ██████████████
██████████████████████████████████
█████████████████████████

██████████████████████████████████████
██████████████████████████████████████
██████████████████████████████████████
████████ blood █████████████████████████████
██████████████████████████████████████
█████████████████████

Cuts

The consultant says *carcinoma* –
the word a missile – malignant cell
eclipsing the night world
of my organs, my left kidney
an inner ear straining to hear
the whoosh of blood.

He says *we'll cut it out*, as if I'm made
of paper and in a way, I am:
my chart spread out before him.

On the street the air is strange;
my secret's blown. Fag ends stub
the pavement, the *Standard* blasts
Inferno – a tower fixed in flames.

There has to be someone to blame.

★

Each morning I remind myself
I'm ill, place my hand below my ribs
as if I can feel the tumour growing
while pundits churn out clichés –
a ticking time bomb,
a tragedy waiting to happen.

We've become experts on cladding,
demand prison for the council suit
who skimped on safety.

Interns with clipboards stalk me:
I sign away what they'll cut out –
a specimen for the lab – produce
piss and blood for plastic cups.

I want to be all surface, nothing deep.

★

3am. I can't sleep. The news app
beeps disaster: I swipe past children
in orange vests, like ladybirds
huddled against panes. I swipe past
cats in boxes, celebrity selfies,
backlit faces replacing dreams.

On the forum, people share
how the cancer returned, how it spread,
their lives squeezed into my phone.

I have to stop. I'm not where they are
yet. They're an open book
I need to close. I can't know
how it ends. In the world of illness

they have a language of their own.

★

A girl has just received the news:
she's sobbing, family shielding her
from the glare of the waiting room.
Bodies – broken, burned – flash briefly
on TV, the newsreader adjusting
her cardigan, her serious face;

the nurse switches to *Bargain Hunt* –
the Red Team are against the clock
in their quest for hidden treasure.

All of us piled together,
flesh and blood, our maladies
stacked like the pile of dated magazines
beside the moulded plastic chairs –

Kate waving from the cover of *Hello!*

★

The surgeon shows me where
she'll make incisions; she assures me
they'll be small. The nurse jokes:
back in a bikini in no time . . .
The surgeon's finger is light
on my skin, softer

than the men who made
their marks, clumsy fingers sometimes
hard enough to shape a bruise,

a purple tag of conquest that faded
just as they did. This goes deeper –
this woman will reach inside me,
carve out the thing that harms me

and then sew me up.

*

The bodies of girls surround me:
unblemished, flesh glowing
through their sheer summer dresses
as they stumble from the pub
or crowd into a train, laughing,
their slim legs tanned and smooth.

The way they burst the stifling air
with their shining hair and credit cards,
they think they're immune from pain –

they don't know yet they carry it
hidden, beneath the skin,
it's what makes them human . . .
listen to me, a crazy old woman –

is that what I am now?

*

On YouTube Yoko is still young.
She kneels, a pair of silver scissors
glinting at her knees; strangers
are invited to slice away her clothes.
She stares at a point beyond
the camera, beyond our gaze.

The women snip at her sweater.
The men chop larger chunks,
greedy for the reveal.

One man mounts the stage,
slits her thin silk slip in half, like boning
a bird, severs the straps holding her
together. Fear widens her eyes –

she remains completely still.

★

Yoko waits for 'Cut Piece' to begin:
the audience is quiet, everyone
holds their breath. I am staring
into space. I feel like I am praying.
I think of her as she prepares
to offer her body to strangers

while consultants handle me, a piece
of meat, a neat package of guts.
I practise leaving my body:

it's not happening to me,
it's happening to someone else,
someone who's gone viral,
someone whose time is up.

I am sacrificing myself.

★

I spend my days reading people's words
as they attempt to stem their loss,
and I change commas to full stops,
or suggest a better verb.
Who am I to say how they should
write their pain, while I hold

my illness close? I refuse to say
its name: *carcinoma*, like a flower
blossoming inside me.

I refuse the confessional splurge,
the Facebook post, the hospital selfie.
I'm just another body, a statistic,
nothing special. Everyone dies –

get over yourself.

★

Khadija's image flashes on my phone –
aged in tintype, a relic in an archive
but she took this picture months ago,
before she died beside her mother,
Mary, who still believed in healers,
spells to ward off evil.

Khadija made this the old way,
coating the metal plate with lacquer
that darkened to hold her face.

She wears a *grandmuba*, a headdress
like the women in Mary's village,
clasps a flower to her mouth;
words blossom on her tongue:

in this space we breathe.

★

Here we come together:
the surgeon, the anaesthetist and me,
three women unified
by my illness. The room is white,
gleaming – a kind of heaven
where I'll leave myself behind.

Where will I go in these long hours?
Still occupying my body,
parts of me switched to low,

in this space between conscious
and *unconscious* – a shadowed
boundary between two towers,
a knife edge, thin

as a single breath.

★

Those who knew they'd perish
sent final texts to loved ones:
The fire is here, I'm dying.
Tell my sons I love them.
I'm staying with the dogs.
Words evaporate

in the gap that opens
in their absence, a wound
that keeps on weeping.

All those hours at my desk,
while news happened somewhere
else, moving words on a screen.
How can words ever mean enough?

Please pray for us.

★

Post-op. The light is strained, sallow;
a shadow forms, then another,
figures speaking from a mountain:
they say my name. There was a man
trapped inside his body; he blinked
each letter of the alphabet to speak.

My eyes are heavy, shuttered.
I'm an open book
I want to close.

Fire laddered the walls. Those who made it out
called to those still trapped inside,
the distance between them
the length of a goodbye –

I reach my arms up, into air.

The Black Place

after Georgia O'Keeffe

How simply she shows us:
a sweep of the brush, her thin wrist
distilling the spring desert
into shades of ruby and gold.

Is there a black line defining
the yellow, or is it just a trick
of contrast? I see it in this *real* sky,
this *real* ridge, the picture I make

with my eyes, the here and now
of sight. She called it 'The Black Place',
perhaps that's why I want to find
that line, to clarify her phrase;

she was in the desert, high noon,
not a trace of cloud. She pulls my eye
to a darker passage, a depression
shadowed in broad light.

When I look up to the sky
in this real place, where the sun
fires my skin, I see a hill behind a hill,
and then another and another:

the place beyond our vision, the place
inside the cave, where the sun
can never reach. It chills me
just to think it into being.

We'll never find it; as soon as we arrive,
the distance shifts to somewhere else,
we remain in foreground, everything moving
around us, even when we're still.

She found the bellow in a skull,
the swagger in a flower; in turn
her lover made her wrist, her breast
his subject. They lived,

exposed their lives to light, and now
they're gone. The black place she made
remains. She shows me how to find it
here, beyond the ridge.

Notes

p16: 'In Clover' was inspired by 'Four, Five, Six, Seven and Nine Leaf Clover Collection' (1972–present), displayed as part of *Tacita Dean: Landscape* at the Royal Academy in 2018.

p17: 'Train at Night in the Desert' is the title of a 1916 charcoal drawing by Georgia O'Keeffe.

p19: Alonis was the Roman name of the port of Villajoyosa near Alicante in Spain. It is the site of the wreck of a Roman cargo ship which was carrying hundreds of amphorae full of garum (a highly prized fish paste made in Cadiz) when it sank.

p20, 32 and 46: The 'Redaction' poems use as their source text page 5 of the booklet *Understanding Kidney Cancer*, Edition 4.0, April 2017, published by Kidney Cancer UK.

p28: 'The Wayfarer' is based on the painting of the same title by Hieronymus Bosch, c.1500.

p37: 'Jade' borrows phrases from a letter written by Georgia O'Keeffe to Alfred Stieglitz in May 1922, after her visit to the Museum of Fine Arts, Boston, where she was allowed to handle jade from the Asian art collection. She said, 'the surfaces were fine and smooth and cold – but even with the coldness of rock they had the warmth of living human flesh'. According to Wikipedia, 'the English word *jade* is derived from the Spanish term *piedra de ijada* (first recorded in 1565) or "loin stone", from its reputed efficacy in curing ailments of the loins and kidneys'.

p40: 'Frits De Vries's Great Work' is based on Otto Prinsen (1936-2006), a Dutch surrealist artist who suffered a creative crisis and stopped painting. He began to collect WWII paraphernalia from the 1970s until his death. A small selection of his collection is presented in two rooms at the Museum Dr. Guislain in Ghent. The label in the museum describes the installation as 'an attempt to grasp the ungraspable'.

p42: Section 2 of 'Darklight' is informed by the artist Cy Twombly, who used to practise 'blind' drawing at night.

p44: 'Small White Dot' is partly inspired by the Georgia O'Keeffe painting 'Black Abstraction' (1927). O'Keeffe was recalling the experience of an operation; as the anaesthetic began to take effect, she tried to reach up to 'a bright overhead light that seemed to whirl and grow increasingly smaller'.

p50: 'Cut Piece' was an early performance work conceived by Yoko Ono in 1964. In each iteration of the piece, the artist sits alone on a stage, dressed in her best clothes, with a pair of scissors in front of her. The audience is instructed to take turns using the scissors to cut off a small piece of clothing, which they could keep. The version I refer to in 'Cuts' is the 1965 performance at Carnegie Recital Hall in New York, available on YouTube.

p51: Khadija Saye was a Gambian-British photographer who died in the Grenfell Tower fire in 2017. A series of photographs entitled 'Dwelling: in this space we breathe', based on Gambian spiritual practices, was shown in the Diaspora Pavilion at the 2017 Venice Biennale.

Acknowledgements

Some of these poems first appeared in the following online or print journals: *Ambit, Anthropocene, Blue of Noon, English, The Harlequin, Long Poem Magazine, Magma, Molly Bloom, New European Review, Poetry & All That Jazz, PN Review, Shearsman Magazine, The Spectator, Tentacular.*

'City', a free translation of a poem by Angel Gonzalez, was included in *A Festschrift for Tony Frazer*, published online in 2015.

'Alice in Hell' was commissioned for the anthology *Alice: Ekphrasis at the British Library* (Joy Lane Publishing, 2016).

'Body Language' appeared in *The Long White Thread of Words: Poems for John Berger* (Smokestack Books, 2016).

'Darklight' was commissioned by Bill Jackson for his film cycle *North by East* in 2017.

Two poems were commissioned for the exhibition *Little Clown, My Heart* at ArthouSE1 in 2018: 'Heart Burn' (inspired by Nadège Mériau's photographic work, 'The Betrayal Bond') and 'Walk All Over Me' (informed by the installation of the same title by Poppy Whatmore).

'Occupation Road' was included in *The Valley Press Anthology of Prose Poetry* (2019).

My thanks to early readers of this book – Anne Berkeley, Claire Crowther, Tim Dooley, Annie Freud, Sue Rose and Siriol Troup – for their invaluable suggestions. And my gratitude to Alison Gill, whose drawings inspired the poems 'Girl', 'Anti-midas' and 'The Lambeth Prophecy'.

And thanks to Amy Wack for her continuing support.